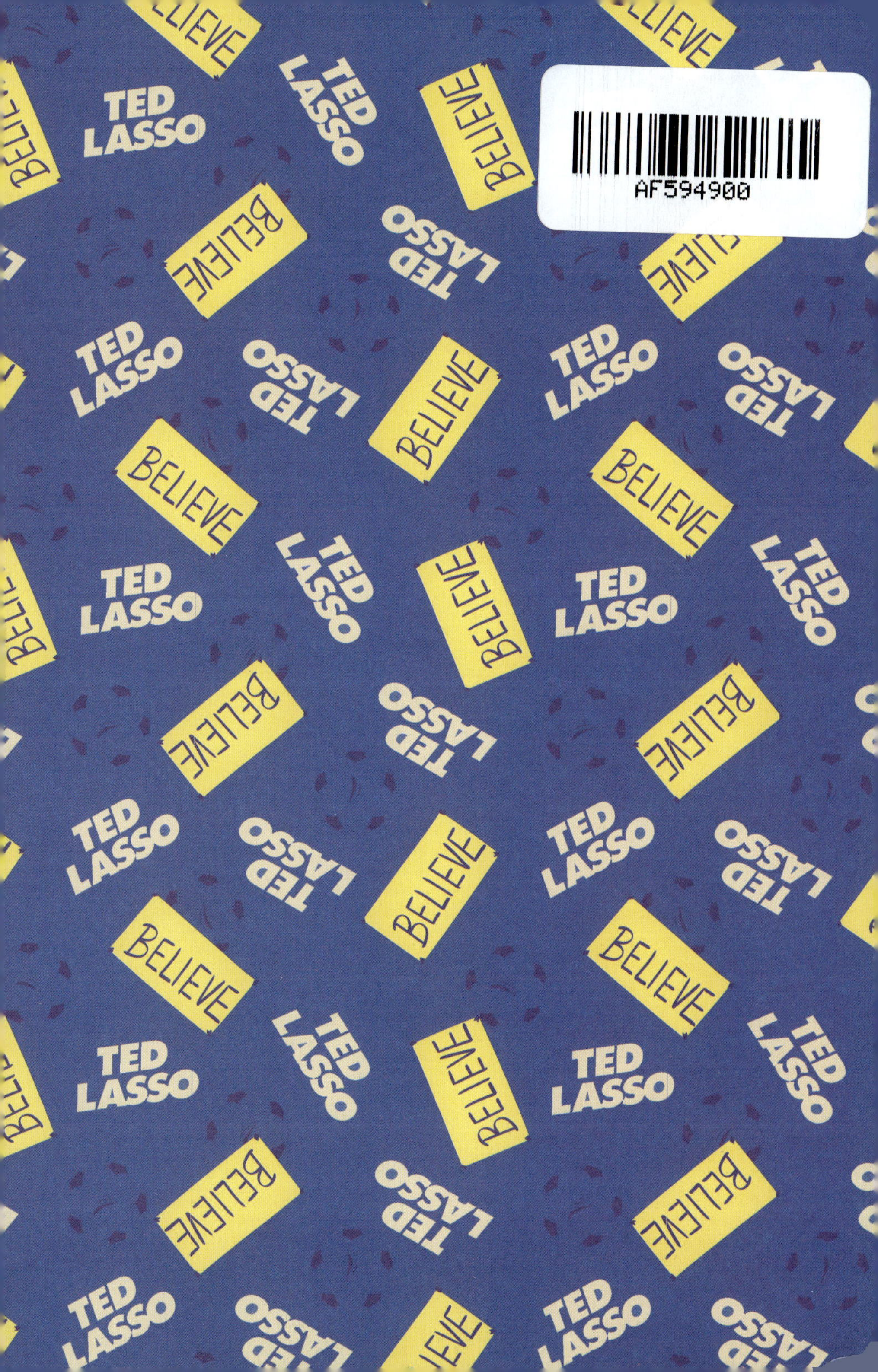
TED LASSO
BELIEVE

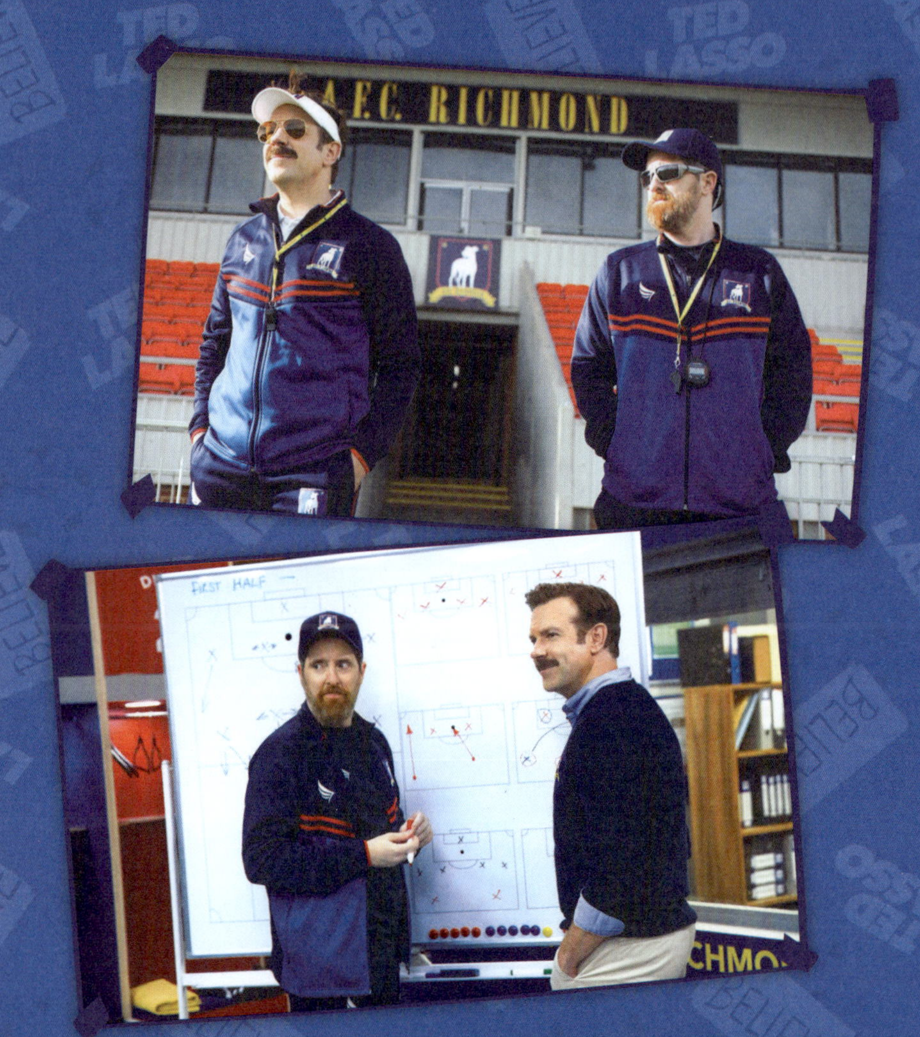

THIS JOURNAL BELONGS TO:

____

I HAVE A HARD TIME HEARING PEOPLE WHO DON'T BELIEVE IN THEMSELVES.

—Ted Lasso

Season 1, Episode 3, "Trent Crimm: The Independent"

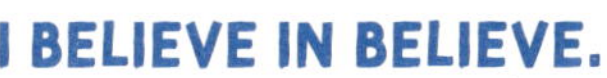
I BELIEVE IN BELIEVE.

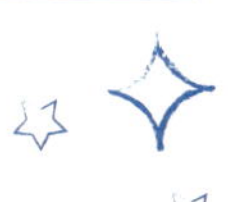

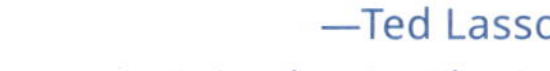
—Ted Lasso

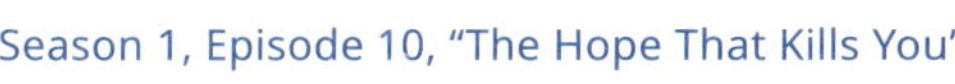
Season 1, Episode 10, “The Hope That Kills You”

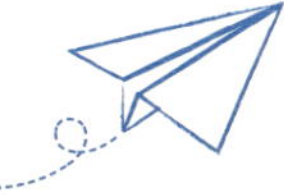

I THINK THAT YOU MIGHT BE SO SURE THAT YOU'RE ONE IN A MILLION, THAT SOMETIMES YOU FORGET THAT OUT THERE YOU'RE JUST ONE IN ELEVEN.

—Ted Lasso

Season 1, Episode 2, "Biscuits"

REBECCA: OH, DO YOU BELIEVE IN GHOSTS, TED?

TED: I DO. BUT MORE IMPORTANTLY, I THINK THEY NEED TO BELIEVE IN THEMSELVES. YOU KNOW?

—Ted Lasso and Rebecca Welton
Season 1, Episode 1, “Pilot”

YOU DON'T NEED TO BE BEST FRIENDS TO BE GREAT TEAMMATES.

—Ted Lasso

Season 1, Episode 4, "For the Children"

BE CURIOUS. NOT JUDGMENTAL.

—Ted Lasso

Season 1, Episode 8, "The Diamond Dogs"

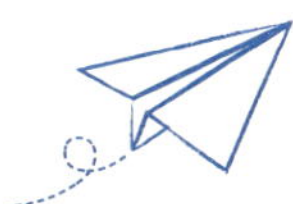

ISN'T THE IDEA OF "NEVER GIVE UP" ONE OF THEM THINGS WE ALWAYS TALK ABOUT IN SPORTS? AND SHOULDN'T THAT APPLY TO PEOPLE TOO?

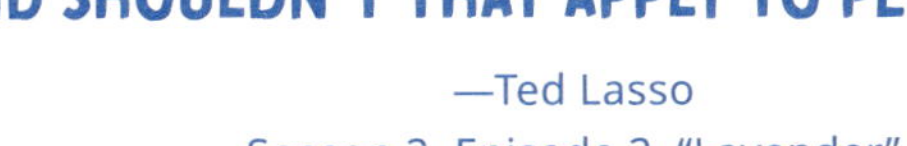

—Ted Lasso
Season 2, Episode 2, "Lavender"

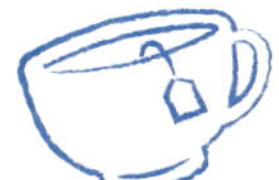

JAMIE: COACH, I'M ME. WHY WOULD I WANT TO BE ANYTHING ELSE?

TED: I'M NOT SURE YOU REALIZE HOW PSYCHOLOGICALLY HEALTHY THAT ACTUALLY IS.

—Jamie Tartt and Ted Lasso
Season 1, Episode 2, "Biscuits"

I WANT YOU TO KNOW THAT I VALUE EACH OF YOUR OPINIONS. EVEN WHEN THEY'RE WRONG.

—Ted Lasso

Season 1, Episode 9, "All Apologies"

IF THAT'S A JOKE, I LOVE IT. IF NOT, CAN'T WAIT TO UNPACK THAT WITH YOU LATER.

—Ted Lasso
Season 1, Episode 1, "Pilot"

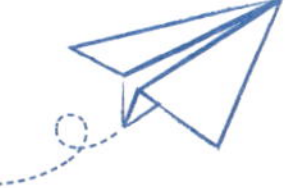

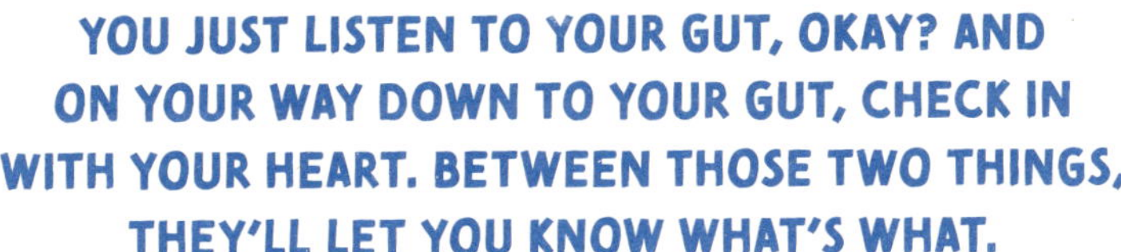

YOU JUST LISTEN TO YOUR GUT, OKAY? AND ON YOUR WAY DOWN TO YOUR GUT, CHECK IN WITH YOUR HEART. BETWEEN THOSE TWO THINGS, THEY'LL LET YOU KNOW WHAT'S WHAT.

—Ted Lasso

Season 2, Episode 11, "Midnight Train to Royston"

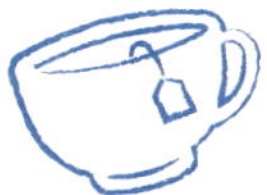

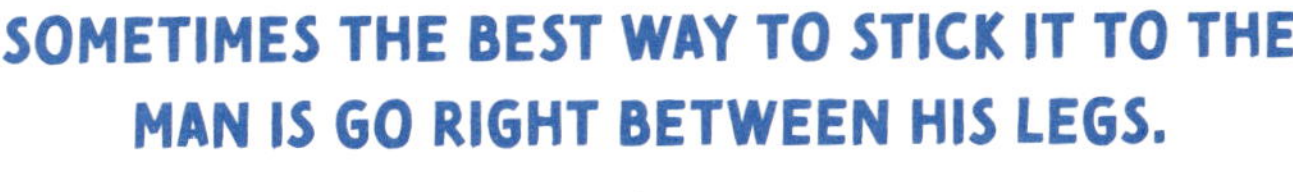

SOMETIMES THE BEST WAY TO STICK IT TO THE MAN IS GO RIGHT BETWEEN HIS LEGS.

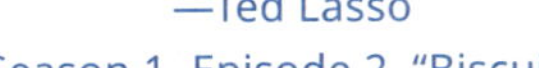

—Ted Lasso

Season 1, Episode 2, "Biscuits"

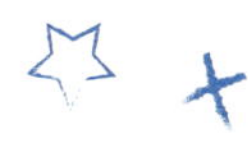

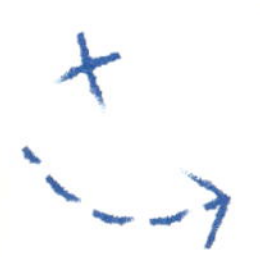

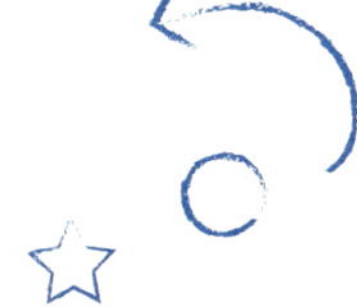

SMELLS LIKE POTENTIAL.

—Ted Lasso
Season 1, Episode 1, "Pilot"

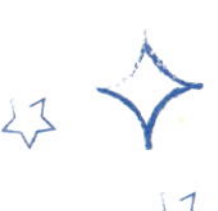

HEY, DOING THE RIGHT THING IS NEVER THE WRONG THING.

—Ted Lasso

Season 2, Episode 3, "Do the Right-est Thing"

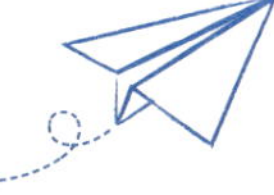

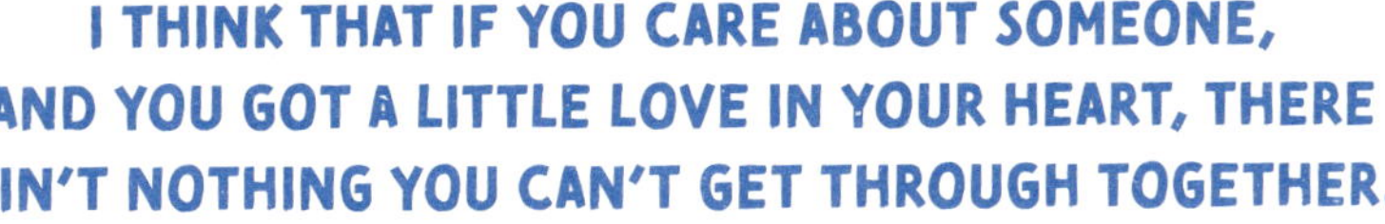

I THINK THAT IF YOU CARE ABOUT SOMEONE, AND YOU GOT A LITTLE LOVE IN YOUR HEART, THERE AIN'T NOTHING YOU CAN'T GET THROUGH TOGETHER.

—Ted Lasso
Season 1, Episode 9, "All Apologies"

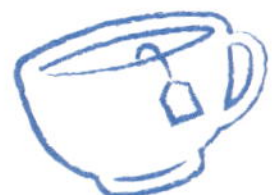

TED: YOU KNOW WHAT TO DO WITH TOUGH COOKIES, DON'T YA?

REBECCA: NO.

TED: DIP 'EM IN MILK.

—Ted Lasso and Rebecca Welton
Season 1, Episode 3, "Trent Crimm: The Independent"

MOST OF THE TIME CHANGE IS A GOOD THING, AND I THINK THAT'S WHAT IT'S ALL ABOUT— EMBRACING CHANGE, BEING BRAVE, DOING WHATEVER YOU HAVE TO SO THAT EVERYONE IN YOUR LIFE CAN MOVE FORWARD WITH THEIRS . . .

—Ted Lasso
Season 1, Episode 5, "Tan Lines"

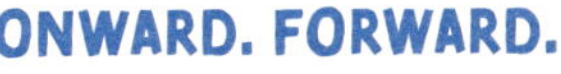

ONWARD. FORWARD.

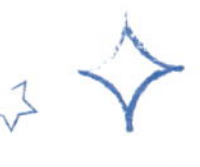

—Ted Lasso

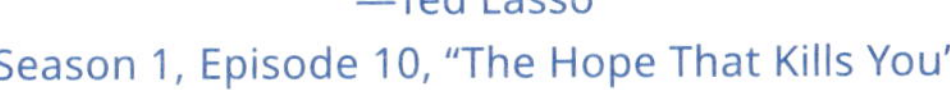

Season 1, Episode 10, "The Hope That Kills You"

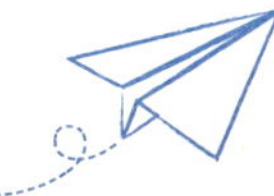

LIVING IN THE MOMENT IS A GIFT.
THAT'S WHY THEY CALL IT THE PRESENT, Y'ALL.

—Ted Lasso
Season 2, Episode 7, "Headspace"

YOU KNOW WHAT THE HAPPIEST ANIMAL ON EARTH IS? IT'S A GOLDFISH. YOU KNOW WHY? [IT'S] GOT A TEN-SECOND MEMORY. BE A GOLDFISH, SAM.

—Ted Lasso
Season 1, Episode 2, "Biscuits"

AS THE MAN ONCE SAID, THE HARDER YOU WORK, THE LUCKIER YOU GET.

—Ted Lasso
Season 1, Episode 1, "Pilot"

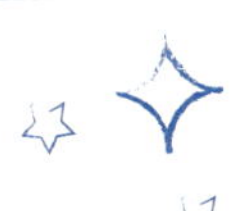

WE MAY NOT HAVE WON,
BUT Y'ALL DEFINITELY SUCCEEDED.

—Ted Lasso

Season 1, Episode 10, "The Hope That Kills You"

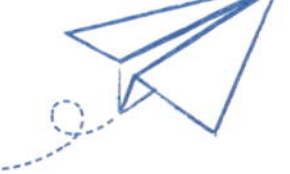

THERE'S TWO BUTTONS I NEVER LIKE TO HIT, ALL RIGHT? AND THAT'S PANIC AND SNOOZE.

—Ted Lasso

Season 2, Episode 1, "Goodbye Earl"

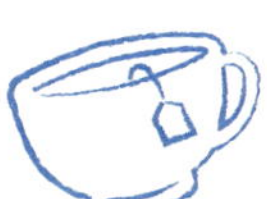

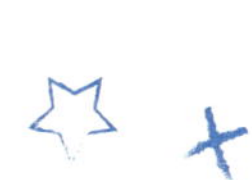

WELL, YOU KNOW, I'VE HEARD THAT TUNE BEFORE, BUT HERE I AM, STILL DANCING.

—Ted Lasso

Season 1, Episode 1, "Pilot"

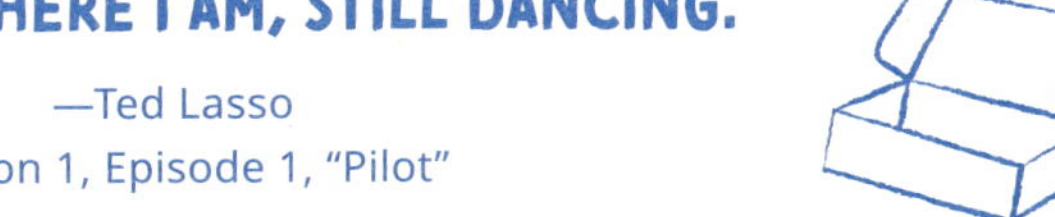

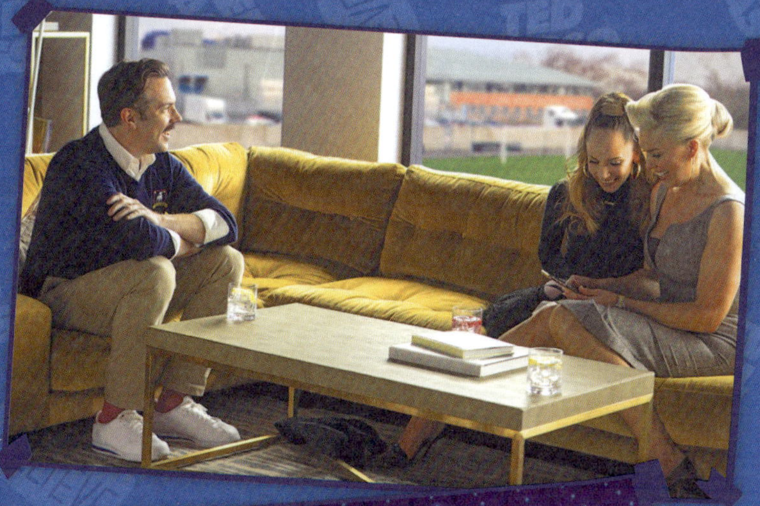

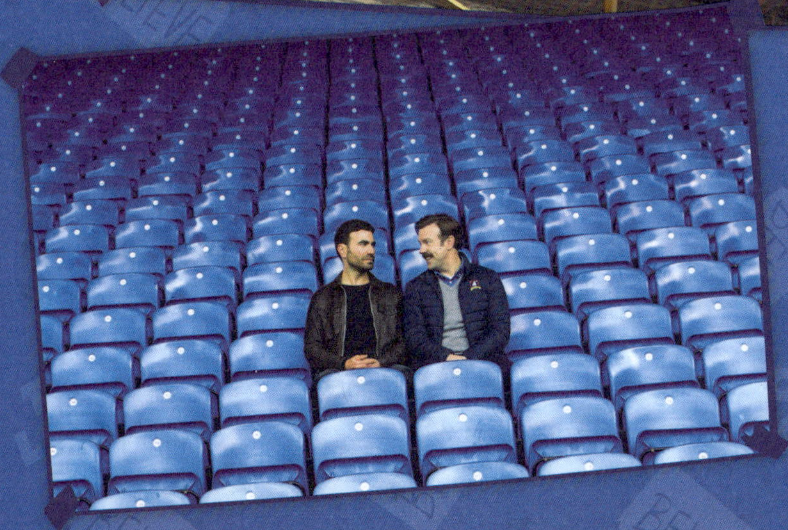

INSIGHTS
www.insighteditions.com

MANUFACTURED IN CHINA
10 9 8 7 6 5 4 3 2 1

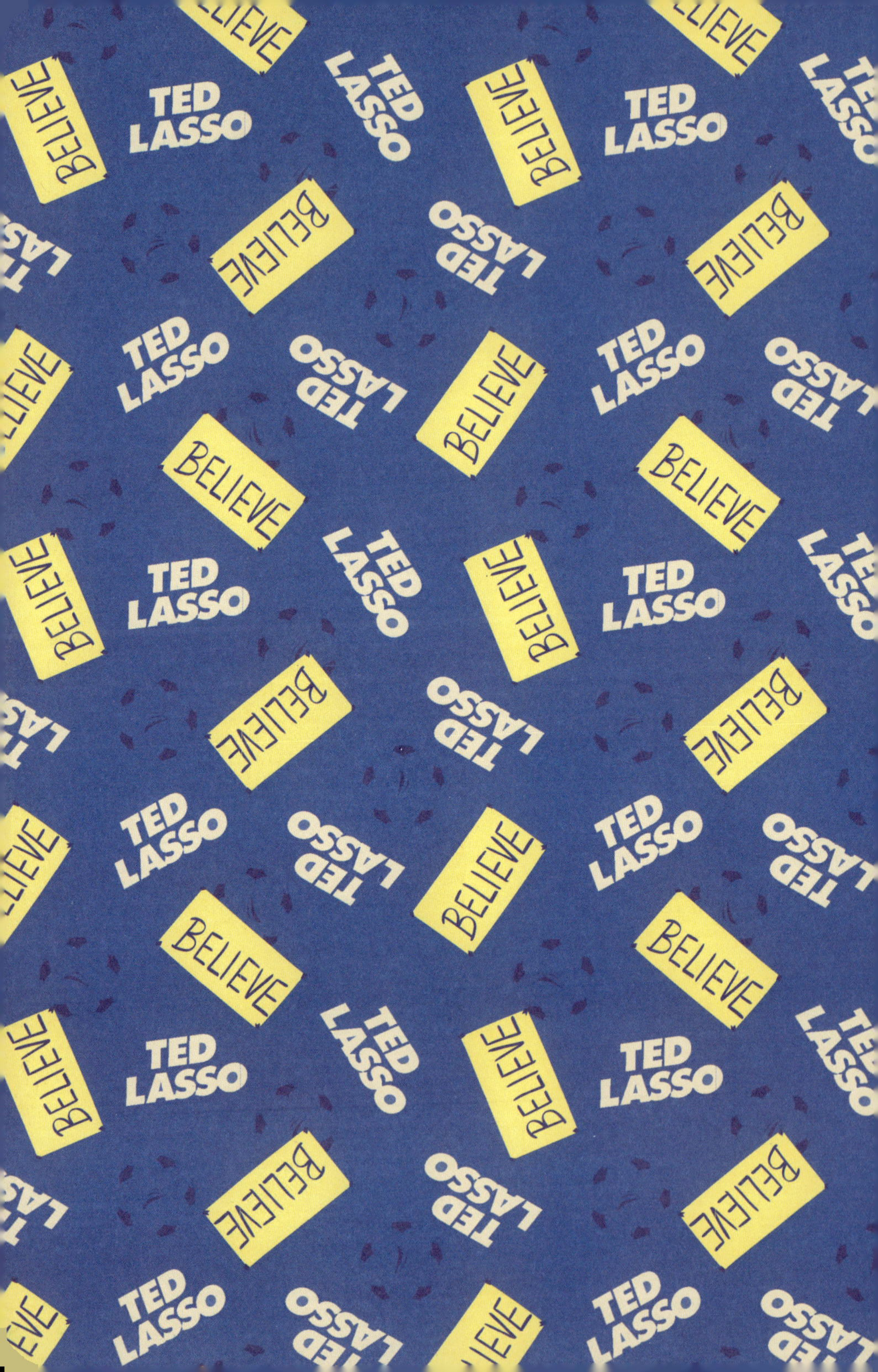
TED LASSO
BELIEVE